BASIC

POWER WORKBOOK

TRUE COLORS

An EFL Course for Real Communication

JAY MAURER

IRENE E. SCHOENBERG

Joan Saslow

Series Director

D1523511

Longman

longman.com

True Colors: An EFL Course for Real Communication
Basic Power Workbook

© 2004 by Pearson Education, Inc.
All rights reserved.
No part of this publication may be reproduced,
stored in a retrieval system, or transmitted
in any form or by any means, electronic, mechanical,
photocopying, recording, or otherwise,
without the prior permission of the publisher.

Pearson Education, 10 Bank Street, White Plains, NY 10606

Workbook by Angela Blackwell
Power Activities by Sarah Lynn
Test-Taking Skills by Ken Sheppard and Angela Castro

Editorial directors: Allen Ascher, Pam Fishman
Senior acquisitions editor: Marian Wassner
Development editors: Barbara Barysh, Trish Lattanzio, Julie Rouse,
Director of design and production: Rhea Banker
Executive managing editor: Linda Moser
Marketing manager: Bruno Paul
Production manager: Ray Keating
Senior production editors: Michael Kemper, Kathleen Silloway
Photo research: Aerin Csigay
Cover design: Rhea Banker, Ann France
Text design: Word & Image Design, Ann France
Text composition: TSI Graphics, Inc.
Senior manufacturing buyer: Edith Pullman
Text font: 11/13 Stone Serif
Text art: Pierre Berthiaume, Moffitt Cecil, Brian Hughes,
   Paul McCusker, Duśan Petricic, Stephen Quinlan, Teco Rodrigues,
   Jill Wood
Photo credits: Gilbert Duclos, Jessica Miller

ISBN: 0-13-184605–1

LONGMAN ON THE **WEB**

Longman.com offers online resources for
teachers and students. Access our Companion
Websites, our online catalog, and our local
offices around the world.

Visit us at **longman.com**.

Printed in the United States of America
1 2 3 4 5 6 7 8 9 10—BAH—08 07 06 05 04 03

Contents

●●

To the Teacher

The *True Colors Power Workbooks* contain two types of activities that students may do in class or at home.

The **Workbook** sections contain numerous opportunities for written reinforcement of the language taught in the Student's Book. They include a variety of written exercises and activities that give students additional practice in this language. Abundant illustrations serve as prompts. The all-new *Power Activities* that appear as the last two pages of every unit provide a step up in the level of challenge. They focus primarily on grammar and emphasize meaningful and personalized practice. Special *Power Writing* activities give students open-ended or free-response writing practice and usually incorporate grammatical structures taught in the unit.

Two **Test-Taking Skills** sections appear in each *True Colors Power Workbook:* one after Unit 5 and one after Unit 10. The questions in these sections are designed to introduce students to the question types and formats they will encounter on the TOEFL and other official examinations while following the language taught at each level of *True Colors.* Although the questions in the **Test-Taking Skills** sections do not replicate the TOEFL or any other official test, they can help prepare students for those tests. A chart describing the questions provided in these sections appears on the next page.

Answers to exercises and activities (except personalized and free-response activities) in both the **Workbook** and the **Test-Taking Skills** sections appear on the *True Colors Companion Website* at **www.longman.com/truecolors**.

Test-Taking Skills

Question Category	Question Objective	Question Format
Vocabulary You Should Know (All levels)	Questions test students' knowledge of words taught as active vocabulary in corresponding units of *True Colors*.	Sentence(s) with a space and 4 possible answers. Students must choose the answer that best completes each sentence.
Vocabulary from Context (All levels)	Questions test students' ability to guess from context the meaning of words they do *not* know.	Sentence(s) with an underlined word and 4 possible answers. Students must choose the answer that is closest in meaning to the underlined word.
Sentence Structure (All levels)	Questions test students' ability to recognize correctly structured sentences.	Sentence(s) with a space and 4 possible answers. Students must choose the answer that best completes each sentence.
Error Correction (All levels)	Questions test students' ability to recognize common grammatical errors.	Sentence with 4 underlined words. Students must choose the underlined word that is *not* correct.
Reading: Main Ideas (Levels 1–4)	Questions test students' ability to recognize the main idea of a passage. Questions may ask about the *topic, title,* or *main idea.*	Question and 4 answer choices. Students read the passage and circle the answer that states the main idea (and not a detail) of the passage.
Reading: Confirming Content (Levels 1–4)	Questions test students' ability to understand details in a passage. Questions may ask about what is *stated* or *indicated* in the passage or what is true according to the passage.	Question and 4 answer choices. Students circle the letter of the answer that gives the correct information from the passage.
Reading: Making Inferences (Levels 3, 4)	Questions test students' ability to make inferences based on information in the passage. Questions may ask about what conclusions can be drawn about the passage, or what is *likely* or *possible* based on information in the passage.	Question and 4 answer choices. Students circle the letter of the answer that is based on information implied in the passage (but not directly stated in the passage).

I'm a student.

1 ## Write the sentences.

Look at the pictures. Write the correct sentence.

| This is Helen. | ~~Hi. I'm Ken.~~ | Nice to meet you, Helen. I'm Julie. |

1. _____Hi. I'm Ken._____

2. _____

3. _____

2 Unscramble the letters.

Look at the pictures. Write the occupations.

1. TESUNTD

She's a ___student___.

2. KAMOHREEM

She's a _____.

3. TRIWER

He's a _____.

4. SRUNE

She's a _____.

5. TODORC

She's a _____.

6. SUBMISSNANE

He's a _____.

7. SERGIN

He's a _____.

❸ Write the answers.

A. *Look at the pictures. Answer the questions.*

1. 

Is she a teacher?

Yes, she is.

2. 

Is he a teacher?

No, he's not. He's a nurse.

3. 

Is she a businesswoman?

____

4. 

Is she an artist?

____

5. 

Is she a singer?

____

6. 

Is he a nurse?

____

7. 

Is he an athlete?

____

8. 

Is he an actor?

____

B. *What do you do? Write about your occupation. Use short answers.*

1. Are you a teacher?

____

2. Are you a student?

____

4 Read and match.

Complete the conversations. Match the sentences.

1. __b__ Are you a student?
2. ____ Hi. I'm Jeff.
3. ____ This is Don Waters.
4. ____ What do you do?
5. ____ Nice to meet you.
6. ____ Is John a writer?
7. ____ Is Ellen an artist?

a. Nice to meet you, too.
b. Yes, I am.
c. Hello, Jeff. I'm Diana.
d. Yes, he is.
e. No, she's not. She's a teacher.
f. I'm a nurse. What about you?
g. Hi, Don. Nice to meet you.

5 Complete the conversation.

Complete the sentences with words from the box.

am	an	I'm	you	Are	is	do

A: Hi! __Are__ you Janet?
     1.

B: Yes, I _____.
         2.

A: Nice to meet you, Janet. _____ Joshua Kahn.
                                    3.

B: Nice to meet _____, too. _____ you a student?
                  4.   **5.**

A: No, _____ not. _____ a teacher.
        6.   **7.**

B: Oh!

A: And this _____ Jack Wesley.
              8.

B: Nice to meet _____, Jack. What _____ you do?
                  9.   **10.**

C: I'm _____ engineer.
        11.

POWER ACTIVITIES

1 Occupations

Look at the picture. Read about the people. Then write the correct name on the line.

Barry's a businessman.

John is an artist.

Ellen's a doctor.

Amy is a singer.

_____ _____ _____ _____
  1.   2.   3.   4.

2 Scrambled Sentences

Unscramble the sentences.

1. nurse / a / is / She /.   *She is a nurse.*_____

2. athlete / you / Are / an /?   _____

3. businessman / a / is / Juan /.   _____

4. a / I'm / writer /.   _____

5. artist / Meg / Is / an /?   _____

3 Mistakes

Find one mistake in each sentence. Then rewrite the sentence correctly.

1. I'm teacher.   *I'm a teacher.*_____

2. Are Janet a student?   _____

3. She's a engineer.   _____

4. He a doctor.   _____

5. Are you actor?   _____

4 Social Language

Choose your response. Circle the letter.

1. Are you a student?

    a. No, I'm not.   **b.** Yes, she is.

2. Hi. I'm Lynn.

    a. Nice to meet you too.   **b.** Nice to meet you, Lynn.

3. What do you do?

    a. I'm Elaine.   **b.** I'm a teacher.

4. Are you Ted?

    a. No, I'm not. I'm Joe.   **b.** Yes, I am. I'm Joe.

5. Is he a writer?

    a. No, he's not. He's a teacher.   **b.** I'm an artist.

SUPER Challenge

5 Power Writing: Introductions and Occupations

Look at the pictures. Write a conversation between Jim and Sue.

Jim: ___Hi. I'm Jim._____

Sue: _____

Jim: _____

Sue: _____

Jim: _____

Sue: _____

Unit 2

Who are they?

① **Write the answers.**

Look at the picture. Answer the questions. Use short answers.

1. Is the old man single?

No, he's not.

2. Is the boy tall?

Yes, he is.

3. Is the woman young?

_____

4. Is the boy old?

_____

5. Is the old woman short?

_____

6. Is the artist good?

_____

❷ Write the names.

Look at the picture. Read about the people. Write the correct name.

_____	_____	*Emma*	_____	_____	_____	_____	_____
1.	**2.**	**3.**	**4.**	**5.**	**6.**	**7.**	**8.**

  My name is Emma. This is a picture of my family and friends.
  My husband is Jack. He's tall. My father is Cesar. He's old. Jim is my son.
He's an athlete. My daughter Sarah is married. My daughter Aida is single.
Gary and Sharon are my neighbors. Gary is an engineer. Sharon is a nurse.

❸ Complete the sentences.

*Complete the sentences with **am**, **are**, or **is**. Use contractions if possible.*

1. Hi, Sue. I'*m*____ Adam.

2. This __*is*__ my teacher.

3. _____ you a student, Peter?

4. The two girls _____ my friends.

5. My doctor _____ a woman.

6. I _____ a singer.

7. This _____ Maria. She _____ my neighbor.

8. _____ you an artist?

9. _____ Jack single?

10. They _____ married.

4 Complete the conversations.

Look at the pictures. Circle the correct words.

Is (**1.** his / (your)) name Joan?

No. (**2.** Our / My) name is Barbara.

a.

This is (**3.** my / your) sister. And this is (**4.** his / our) father.

Nice to meet you.

b.

This is (**5.** his / my) father. And this is (**6.** her / his) friend.

c.

Is she (**7.** your / my) sister?

No. She's (**8.** his / my) neighbor. And he's (**9.** her / his) husband.

d.

5 Unscramble the conversation.

Number the sentences 1, 2, 3 . . . .

_____ And this is his wife, Jean.

_____ Great. Linda, this is my classmate, Robbie.

_____ Hi, Robbie. Nice to meet you.

_____ Oh, hi, Dave! How are you doing?

___1___ Hi, Linda!

_____ Hello, Jean.

_____ Nice to meet you, too.

6 Complete the sentences.

*Write **Who** or **What**.*

1. __What__'s your name?

2. __Who__'s your teacher?

3. _____'s her name?

4. _____'s the singer?

5. _____'s your phone number?

6. _____ are the teachers?

7. _____'s Bob?

7 Complete the chart.

Complete the chart about your family and friends.

	name	man	woman	boy	girl	athlete	student	young	old	tall	short
(mother)/ father	Mary		✔					✔		✔	
sister / brother											
neighbor											
friend											
wife / husband											

8   UNIT 2

8 Write the answers.

A. *Answer the questions.*

Example:	What's your name?	Jane Donovan.

1. What's your name? _____

2. What's your phone number? _____

3. Are you single? _____

4. Are you married? _____

5. Who's your English teacher? _____

B. *Now write a paragraph. Use your answers from **A**.*

Example:

My name is Jane Donovan. My phone number
is 579-7743. I'm single. . . .

_____

_____

_____

_____

_____

POWER ACTIVITIES

1 Sentence Correction

Look at the pictures. Correct the false statements.

1. Julie is a woman.

No, she's not. She's a girl.

2. They are neighbors.

_____

3. Diane is a good athlete.

_____

4. Steve is short.

_____

Steve   Joe

5. Kevin is a young man.

_____

2 *Who* and *What* Questions

*Look at the answers. Then write questions with **Who** or **What**.*

1. A: _What's her name_____ ?

B: Her name is Anne.

2. A: _____ ?

B: They're Tony and Steve.

3. A: _____ ?

B: Danielle Cho.

4. A: _____ ?

B: It's 412-6415.

5. A: _____ ?

B: He's a singer.

③ A Family Tree

*Look at Jack's family tree. Then complete the sentences with **My, His, Her, Our,** or **Their.***

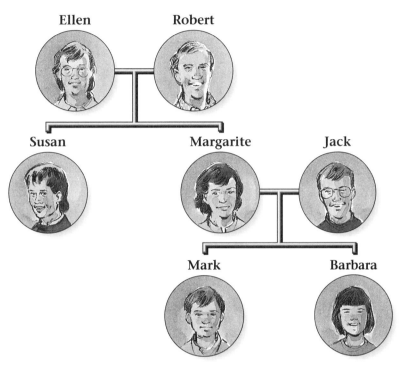

Ellen   Robert

Susan   Margarite   Jack

Mark   Barbara

_____My_____ name is Jack. I'm an engineer. _____ wife's name is Margarite. She's a
   1.   **2.**

doctor. _____ father's name is Robert. He's a businessman. _____ wife is Ellen.
           3.   **4.**

_____ other daughter is Susan. She's single. _____ wife and I have two children.
   5.   **6.**

_____ son's name is Mark. _____ sister's name is Barbara. They're students.
   7.   **8.**

SUPER Challenge

④ Power Writing: Your Family

Now write about your family. Use possessive adjectives.

_____

_____

_____

_____

_____

Unit 3

Where is Bob?

① Label the pictures.

Label the pictures with words from the box.

the gym	the library	~~the bank~~	the supermarket	the post office

1. _the bank_

2. _____

3. _____

4. _____

5. _____

❷ Label the pictures.

Label the pictures with words from the box. Use **a** or **an**.

beautiful	big	expensive	old	~~tall~~
watch	belt	ring	~~man~~	woman

1. _a tall man_

2. _____

3. _____

4. _____

5. _____

❸ Complete the sentences.

A. Complete the conversations with **He**, **She**, **It**, or **They**. Use contractions.

1. A: Where's Emily?

  B: _She's_ at the gym.

2. A: Where's the post office?

  B: _It's_ on Walnut Street.

3. A: Where's John?

  B: _____ at the bank.

4. A: Where's your apartment?

  B: _____ on Union Street.

5. A: Where are the boys?

  B: _____ at the supermarket.

6. A: Where's your mother?

  B: _____ at work.

B. *Now look at the pictures. Answer the questions.*

1.

Where's Tom?

He's at the bank.

2.

Where's the library?

It's on Park Avenue.

3.

Where's Jason?

_____

4.

Where are Bill and Ben?

_____

5.

Where's Diana?

_____

6.

Where's the house?

_____

7.

Where's the post office?

_____

8.

Where are the students?

_____

4 Read and match.

Match the questions and the answers.

1. __f__ Hello. How are you doing?
2. _____ What's your name?
3. _____ Where are you from?
4. _____ Are you a businessman?
5. _____ Are you married?
6. _____ That's a nice briefcase. Is it from Italy?

a. I'm from New York.

b. No. I'm single.

c. Dennis McCarthy.

d. No. It's from Japan.

e. No, I'm not. I'm a writer.

f. I'm fine.

5 Write the answers.

Look at the business cards. Answer the questions.

ILT Technology

Kim Hastings
Engineer

324 Lombard St.
Philadelphia, PA 19107
U.S.A.
Tel. (215) 862-7878

Felipe Martins
Artist

Rua Paraiso, 168
04004-000 São Paulo-SP
Brazil
Tel. (011) 5584-2408

1. Is Kim from Japan?　　　　No, she's not.

2. Where's Kim from?　　　　She's from the United States.

3. Is Kim a businesswoman?

4. What's her phone number?

5. What's her address?

6. Where's Felipe from?

7. What's his phone number?

8. Is he a student?

6 Complete the puzzle.

Complete the sentences.

CLUES

Across

1. **A:** ___How___'s it going?

   B: Great.

3. This is a _____ watch.

6. Chris is not a boy; she's a _____.

9. He's not a student; he's a _____.

12. She's not a nurse; she's a _____.

14. He's at _____ bank.

15. This is my daughter. And this is my _____.

16. I'm not a teacher; I'm a _____.

18. _____'s your name?

Down

2. This is a _____.

4. I'm = I _____.

5. _____. I'm Ken.

7. **A:** _____'s Leroy?

   B: He's at school.

8. Anne is my sister, and Charles is my _____.

10. She's an _____.

11. **A:** Who are they?

    B: Jane and _____ husband.

12. **A:** What _____ you do?

    B: I'm a homemaker.

13. The post office is _____ Main Street.

17. Nice _____ meet you.

POWER ACTIVITIES

① Places

*Complete each sentence with **at** or **on**.*

1. The bank is _____on_____ Main Street.

2. The gym is _____ Water Street.

3. My husband is _____ home.

4. Her classmates are _____ school.

5. Our apartment is _____ Center Avenue.

6. The boys are _____ the stadium.

7. My friends are _____ the beautiful theater _____ Maple Avenue.

8. The new post office is _____ Oak Street.

② Sentence Correction

Look at the pictures. Rewrite each sentence as a negative statement. Then correct the sentence.

1. They're at the library.

They're not at the library. They're at the gym.

2. His brother is an engineer.

_____

3. The bank is on Grove Street.

Main Street

_____

4. The wallet is cheap.

$120.⁰⁰

_____

5. Kim's brother is short.

_____

❸ *Where* Questions

*Look at the answers. Then write questions with **Where**.*

1. A: _Where is she_____?

  B: She's at the post office.

2. A: _____?

  B: It's on Peach Street.

3. A: _____?

  B: We're in our apartment.

4. A: _____?

  B: At the supermarket.

5. A: _____?

  B: In the library.

6. A: _____?

  B: They're on Elm Avenue.

SUPER Challenge

❹ Power Writing: Your City

Answer the questions about places in your city.

1. Where is the post office? _____

2. Where is the public library? _____

3. Where is the hospital? _____

4. Where is your house / apartment? _____

5. Where is your supermarket? _____

6. Where is your bank? _____

When is the movie?

❶ Label the pictures.

Label the pictures with words from the box.

| a movie | a play | a soccer game | a concert | a party | ~~a dance~~ |

1.

   a dance

2.

   _____

3.

   _____

4. _____

5. _____

6. _____

❷ Read and match.

Look at the calendar. Complete the sentences.

Today is Thursday.

Week at a Glance		
	Morning	**Afternoon**	**Evening**
THURSDAY		3:00 soccer game	8:00 play at Lyric Theater
FRIDAY			7:30 dance
SATURDAY		2:00 concert, People's Park	9:00 Anita's Party
SUNDAY	11:00 basketball game		7:15 movie with Paula

1. __f__ The soccer game is   a. Saturday afternoon.

2. _____ The movie is   b. tonight.

3. _____ The dance is   c. tomorrow night.

4. _____ The play is   d. Sunday night.

5. _____ The concert is   e. Saturday night.

6. _____ The basketball game is   f. today.

7. _____ The party is   g. Sunday morning.

3 Complete the charts.

Complete the charts. Use words from the box.

April	**August**	**Wednesday**	**fall**	**July**
~~January~~	**March**	~~Sunday~~	~~spring~~	**June**
February	**Thursday**	**Saturday**	**May**	**December**
November	**Monday**	**September**	**winter**	**Friday**
Tuesday	**October**	**summer**		

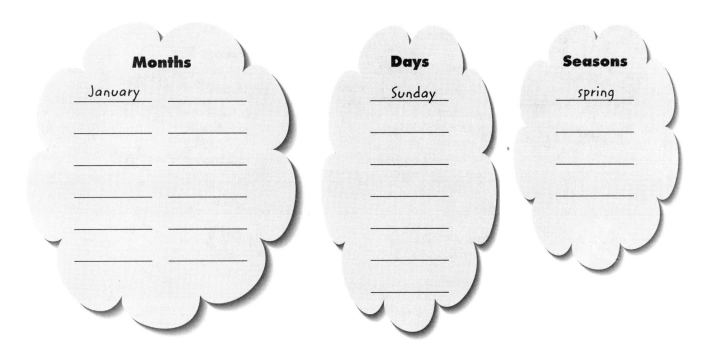

Months

January _____

Days

Sunday

Seasons

spring

4 Unscramble the conversation.

Number the sentences 1, 2, 3 . . . .

_____ Fine. Is Patricia there?

___1___ Hello?

_____ OK. Bye.

_____ No, she's not. She's at a basketball game.

_____ Hi, John. This is Barbara.

_____ Oh, OK. I'll call back later.

_____ Oh, hi, Barbara. How's it going?

5 Write the sentences.

A. *Look at the picture. Correct the false statements.*

1. The party is on Sunday.

   No, it's not. It's on Saturday.

2. The movie is at 7 p.m.

   No, it's not. It's at 8 p.m.

3. The concert is at the stadium.

   _____

4. The concert is on Wednesday night.

   _____

5. The soccer game is on Wednesday.

   _____

6. The movie is at the Lyric Theater.

   _____

B. *Now write three more sentences about the picture.*

1. <u>There's a party on Saturday at 3:00 p.m.</u>

2. _____

3. _____

4. _____

6 Label the pictures.

Look at the pictures. Write sentences from the box.

What time is it?	**Ben? This is Sarah.**	**See you.**
~~**Is Bobby there?**~~	**Uh-oh. I'm late.**	

1. <u>Is Bobby there?</u>

2. _____

3. _____

4. _____

5. _____

POWER ACTIVITIES

1 Questions

Look at the flyers. Read the answers. Then write questions.

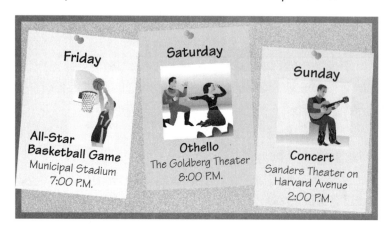

1. A: When is the basketball game _____?

B: It's on Friday night.

2. A: _____?

B: At 7:00.

3. A: _____?

B: The game is at the stadium.

4. A: _____?

B: *Othello.*

5. A: _____?

B: It's at 8:00.

6. A: _____?

B: The concert is at Sanders Theater.

7. A: _____?

B: It's on Harvard Avenue.

8. A: _____?

B: On Sunday afternoon. At 2:00.

❷ Mistakes

Find one mistake in each sentence. Then rewrite the sentence correctly.

1. There is two soccer games today.

   There are two soccer games today.

2. The movie is at Friday night at 7:00 at the Cineplex.

   _____

3. The concert is at the theater on April.

   _____

4. The party is in 6:00.

   _____

5. When the play at the library?

   _____

❸ Power Writing: It's a party!

Write an invitation for a party you are having at your house/apartment.

IT'S A PARTY!

What:

_____

Where:

_____

When:

_____

What time:

_____

He's watching TV.

❶ Write the answers.

Look at the pictures. Answer the questions.

1.

Where is the book?
It's on the table.

2.

Where are Tom and Doris?
They're in the living room.

3.

Where is Paul?

_____

4.

Where's the magazine?

_____

5.

Where is the newspaper?

_____

6.

Where are the letters?

_____

7.

Where is Gina?

_____

8.

Where's the table?

_____

❷ Label the pictures.

A. *Label the pictures with sentences from the box.*

He's reading a newspaper. **They're working.**	**They're eating.** **They're sleeping.**	~~**She's studying.**~~ **He's shaving.**

1.

   She's studying.

2.

   _____

3.

   _____

4.

   _____

5.

   _____

6.

   _____

B. *Now complete the sentences. Use verbs from the box. Use the present continuous tense.*

eat	study	write	read

1.

2.

3.

4.

③ Read and match.

Match the questions and the answers.

A: Hi, Jan. It's Mom. Are you busy?

B: ___b___
____1.____

A: What are you doing?

B: _____
____2.____

A: Is Peter there?

B: _____
____3.____

A: Where are the children?

B: _____
____4.____

A: He's sleeping? Why is he sleeping in the afternoon?

B: _____
____5.____

a. Marta is at a basketball game, and Freddy is sleeping.

b. No, not right now.

c. I don't know!

d. I'm reading the newspaper.

e. No. He's working today.

④ Complete the sentences.

Complete the conversations. Use words from the box.

Who	Where	What	When	What time	Why

1. A: _____*Who*___'s in the kitchen?

B: Rose. She's eating breakfast.

2. A: _____ are you doing?

B: I'm studying.

3. A: _____ are you studying in the kitchen?

B: Because Allen is watching TV in our bedroom.

4. A: _____ is the concert?

B: It's Saturday afternoon.

5. A: _____ is the movie?

B: It's at six-thirty.

6. A: _____ is the party?

B: At my house.

7. A: _____ are the boys doing?

B: They're watching TV.

8. A: _____'s in the bathroom?

B: Jerry. He's shaving.

9. A: _____'s the basketball game?

B: It's at the stadium.

10. A: _____ is it?

B: It's four-fifteen.

⑤ Write the answers.

Look at the picture. Answer the questions.

1. What time is it?

    Five-thirty.   (or 5:30.)

2. Where are Jeff and Kathryn?

    They're in the living room.

3. Is Jeff working?

4. What's he doing?

5. Is Kathryn busy?

6. What's she doing?

7. Where are Sam and Janie?

8. What are they doing?

9. Who's in the bedroom?

10. What's he doing?

POWER ACTIVITIES

1 Present Continuous

Complete the sentences with the present continuous.

1. Is Felix ___*working*___ right now?
work

2. What are they _____?
do

3. Who's _____ TV in the
watch
living room?

4. Is Mary _____ for her test?
study

5. Where are you _____ lunch?
eat

6. Are you _____ to the movies
go
with Sally?

2 Sentence Correction

Look at the pictures. Correct the false statements.

1. Mrs. Robinson is in the bedroom.

She's not in the bedroom. She's in the living room.

2. She is reading a magazine.

_____

3. There are three books on the table.

_____

4. They are in the kitchen.

_____

5. She is eating lunch.

_____

6. He is watching a basketball game.

_____

❸ People and Activities

What are they doing? Write sentences about each person.

1. Matt is studying. _____
_____

Matt

4. _____
_____

Louis

2. _____
_____

Carol

5. _____
_____

Linda

3. _____
_____

Judy

6. _____
_____

Chris

SUPER Challenge

❹ Power Writing: Questions with the Present Continuous

Write four questions you can ask about the pictures in Exercise 3.

Example:
• • • • • •
Is Matt sleeping? _____

1. _____

2. _____

3. _____

4. _____

Review

❶ Read and match.

Complete the conversations. Match the sentences.

1. ___c___ How's it going?		**a.**	Bye.
2. _____ What do you do?		**b.**	Eight-fifteen.
3. _____ Are you busy?		**c.**	Great.
4. _____ This is my wife, Sue.		**d.**	I'm an artist.
5. _____ That's a nice belt. Where's it from?		**e.**	Nice to meet you.
6. _____ Is Martin there?		**f.**	Brazil.
7. _____ See you!		**g.**	No, I'm not. Come in!
8. _____ Who is he?		**h.**	No, she's single.
9. _____ Is she married?		**i.**	No, he's not. He's at a basketball game.
10. _____ What time is it?		**j.**	Ron. He's a doctor.

❷ Write the answers.

Answer the questions.

Example:	What's your name?	Lisa Drummond.

1. What's your name? _____

2. What do you do? _____

3. What time is it right now? _____

4. What are you doing right now? _____

5. What's your phone number? _____

6. Who's your English teacher? _____

7. Where is your English teacher from? _____

❸ Circle the word.

Circle the word that is different.

1.	(father)	artist	actor	singer
2.	brother	father	sister	husband
3.	chair	kitchen	sofa	table
4.	afternoon	morning	night	month
5.	concert	library	movie	play
6.	three	thirty	ninety	forty

❹ Write true or false.

*Read the letter. Write **T** (true) or **F** (false).*

September 16

Dear Mom,
How's it going? I'm fine. School is great. My teachers are all good.
Right now I'm in the kitchen in my new apartment! There's one bedroom, a living
room, and a kitchen. The rooms are small, but the apartment is cheap. My address is
465 Chestnut Street, Apartment 2. My phone number is (904) 552-7906.
Sandy and Marisa are my neighbors. They're students too. Sandy's from New York.
Marisa's from Texas. Right now, Sandy's at the gym and Marisa's watching TV in the
living room. Marisa and I are good friends.

Lots of love,
Liz

1. __T__ The letter is from Liz.

2. __F__ The letter is to Sandy.

3. _____ Liz is a student.

4. _____ Liz is in her bedroom.

5. _____ The apartment is expensive.

6. _____ The apartment is on Chestnut Street.

7. _____ There are three students in the apartment.

8. _____ Marisa is from New York.

9. _____ Sandy is studying.

10. _____ Marisa is watching TV.

⑤ Complete the puzzle.

A. *Circle nine words for rooms and things. Words are horizontal (→), diagonal (↗), or vertical (↓).*

L	I	V	I	N	G	R	O	O	M
A	K	O	C	H	E	A	P	O	X
D	I	N	I	N	G	R	O	O	M
E	T	A	B	L	E	R	U	T	S
A	C	H	A	L	D	O	S	H	O
S	H	O	W	E	R	R	T	H	U
W	E	L	B	I	T	S	O	F	A
A	N	D	A	R	S	I	V	D	O
O	W	H	T	O	I	L	E	T	W
U	C	P	A	R	O	B	L	U	T

B. *Now write the words here.*

_____ table _____   _____

_____   _____

_____   _____

_____   _____

_____   _____

TEST-TAKING SKILLS

SECTION I
Vocabulary You Should Know

> 1. Read the sentence(s).
> 2. Try each answer in the space.
> 3. Circle the letter of the answer that best completes the sentence.

1. Hi, I'm Anne. I'm _____. What do you do?

   (A) a woman
   (B) a daughter
   (C) an engineer
   (D) a businessman

2. Jack's not a student. He's _____ at General Hospital.

   (A) an artist
   (B) a classmate
   (C) a nurse
   (D) a singer

3. I'm writing a book about Brazil. I'm _____.

   (A) a homemaker
   (B) a writer
   (C) a neighbor
   (D) an athlete

4. Is Ellen _____? Or is she married?

   (A) single
   (B) new
   (C) tall
   (D) short

5. Who is that? Is he your _____?

   (A) wife
   (B) sister
   (C) mother
   (D) husband

6. What's your _____? Is it 232-1748?

   (A) address
   (B) occupation
   (C) name
   (D) phone number

7. The library is on Main Street. It's a tall _____.

   (A) apartment
   (B) house
   (C) building
   (D) stadium

8. That watch is $5,000. It's not cheap. In fact, it is very _____.

   (A) big
   (B) ugly
   (C) expensive
   (D) new

9. The play is tonight at 7:00 p.m. It's at the _____.

   (A) stadium
   (B) gym
   (C) movies
   (D) theater

10. It's Tuesday. Maybe there's a basketball _____ today.

    (A) concert
    (B) play
    (C) dance
    (D) game

11. The concert is _____ Wednesday at seven o'clock. Do you want to go?

    (A) at
    (B) in
    (C) on
    (D) from

12. There's a party Saturday afternoon. It's at _____.

   (A) 11:30 p.m.
   (B) 3:00 p.m.
   (C) 10:00 a.m.
   (D) 2:30 a.m.

13. There's a new _____ in the kitchen.

   (A) shower
   (B) stove
   (C) toilet
   (D) bed

14. Max and Eric aren't studying at the library. They're _____ a movie in the living room.

   (A) watching
   (B) writing
   (C) reading
   (D) eating

15. Is _____ at 9:00 tomorrow morning?

   (A) dinner
   (B) lunch
   (C) spring
   (D) breakfast

SECTION 2
Vocabulary from Context

> 1. Read the sentence(s).
> 2. Try each answer in place of the underlined word(s).
> 3. Circle the letter of the best answer.

1. There's no class this afternoon. The <u>instructor</u> is not at school today. She's at the doctor's with her son.

   (A) nurse
   (B) student
   (C) teacher
   (D) partner

2. What is your wife's <u>job</u> at the hospital? Is she a doctor? A nurse?

   (A) occupation
   (B) address
   (C) event
   (D) relationship

3. My father is <u>an author</u>. Right now he is working on a book about Chicago.

   (A) a singer
   (B) an engineer
   (C) an athlete
   (D) a writer

4. In basketball, the <u>players</u> are usually tall.

   (A) actors
   (B) athletes
   (C) artists
   (D) partners

5. That man is her friend, not her <u>spouse</u>. She's single.

   (A) son
   (B) brother
   (C) husband
   (D) classmate

6. There's nothing to eat for dinner. How about going to the <u>grocery store</u>?

   (A) post office
   (B) bank
   (C) library
   (D) supermarket

7. Ten dollars? Uh-oh. My wallet is in my <u>handbag</u>. And my handbag is at home on the dining room table!

    (A) ring
    (B) purse
    (C) watch
    (D) belt

8. Wow! This ring is only thirty dollars. That isn't expensive at all. In fact, it's very <u>inexpensive</u>.

    (A) bad
    (B) cheap
    (C) old
    (D) big

9. <u>Autumn</u> is the season between summer and winter. In North America, it's in September, October, and November.

    (A) Spring
    (B) July
    (C) Fall
    (D) January

10. There's a soccer <u>match</u> tomorrow. It's at the stadium on Spring Street.

    (A) dance
    (B) play
    (C) concert
    (D) game

11. Are you busy tonight? There's a good <u>film</u> at the Cineplex. The actors are Ben Lopez and Jennifer Damon.

    (A) movie
    (B) game
    (C) concert
    (D) party

12. There's a dinner party Thursday <u>evening</u> at 8:00 p.m.

    (A) morning
    (B) afternoon
    (C) day
    (D) night

13. It's late at night, and the students are in bed. They're <u>asleep</u>, but Jason isn't. He's studying for a test.

    (A) shaving
    (B) working
    (C) sleeping
    (D) talking

14. Amy and her classmate Jan are <u>having</u> pizza in the cafeteria.

    (A) watching
    (B) eating
    (C) reading
    (D) studying

15. The Smiths are looking for a new <u>couch</u> for their living room. They need a big couch for their family of six to sit and watch TV.

    (A) sofa
    (B) stove
    (C) shower
    (D) bed

SECTION 3
Sentence Structure

> 1. Read the sentence(s).
> 2. Try each answer in the space.
> 3. Circle the letter of the answer that best completes the sentence.

1. Her brother is a doctor. _____ working at the hospital right now.

   (A) He
   (B) He's
   (C) Is he
   (D) His

2. The teacher _____ a letter to the students.

   (A) write
   (B) she's writing
   (C) are writing
   (D) is writing

3. _____ the address of your new house?

   (A) When are
   (B) When is
   (C) What are
   (D) What's

4. There's a call for you, Diane. _____ your classmate, David.

   (A) It
   (B) They're
   (C) It's
   (D) Is it

5. Is Bob _____ for the test tomorrow?

   (A) studying
   (B) study
   (C) is studying
   (D) he's studying

6. I'm a writer. _____ books are about professional athletes.

   (A) Their
   (B) Your
   (C) My
   (D) His

7. _____ only twelve students in this class.

   (A) There is
   (B) They're
   (C) Is there
   (D) There are

8. _____ looking for Helen? She's at the movies.

   (A) You
   (B) Are you
   (C) You are
   (D) Your

9. Rosa _____ sleeping. She's eating breakfast.

   (A) is she
   (B) am not
   (C) isn't
   (D) aren't

10. I _____ on the bus to Chicago.

    (A) am
    (B) is
    (C) are
    (D) isn't

11. _____ your sister?

    (A) Where is
    (B) Where are
    (C) Where
    (D) Where is she

12. Why is Jack in the bedroom? Is _____?

    (A) sleeping
    (B) he's sleeping
    (C) he sleeping
    (D) he is sleeping

13. Hector and Julie are reading _____ the kitchen. Margaret is watching a game on TV.

(A) at
(B) in
(C) from
(D) on

14. _____ the man from England?

(A) Who are
(B) He is
(C) Who's
(D) Where are

15. _____ you an engineer or a doctor?

(A) Who's
(B) Are
(C) What's
(D) Is

SECTION 4
Error Correction

> 1. Read the sentence.
> 2. Read the underlined words and the words around them.
> 3. Circle the letter below the word that is not correct.

1. There is a rings on the sink in the bathroom.
      A   B C   D

2. His class is at the library on Tuesday in eight-fifteen.
    A   B   C   D

3. The students is at a basketball game at the stadium on Main Street.
          A B   C   D

4. The husband is shaving, and her wife is writing a letter.
          A   B   C   D

5. There is one hundred small apartments and fifty big apartments in the building
         A   B   C
   on Maple Avenue.
   D

6. Why are your brother sleeping on the sofa in the living room?
    A   B   C   D

7. Mr. Lee is a engineer, but right now he's working at the supermarket.
         A B   C   D

8. Is Peter reading a book, an newspaper, or a magazine?
    A   B   C   D

9. The play is on Saturday at the Lowell Theater, and the concert is on December.
         A B   C   D

10. My classmates are all working on they conversations.
     A   B   C   D

11. I aren't eating lunch right now because Elena's studying in the kitchen.
       A   B   C   D

12. Ana is a busy young businesswomen and student.
         A   B   C   D

13. My school is expensive, my book are expensive, and my apartment is expensive.
        A   B   C   D

14. Are there a doctor from India at your hospital?
     A   B   C   D

15. It's 10 p.m., and Maria and her daughter are watch a movie on TV.
     A   B   C   D

❶ Label the pictures.

Look at the pictures. Write the names of the foods and drinks.

Example:

    __fi sh__

1.   m_____

2.   _____t

3.   ____i_____

4.   _____p

5.   r_____

6.   c_____

7.   ____t_____

8.   ____s____

9.   ____r_____

10.   _____s

11.   a s_____

12.   ____ c_____

❷ Complete the sentences.

A. Complete the sentences with the correct form of the verb.

1. I __like__ eggs with toast.
    like / likes

2. We _____ bread and milk.
    need / needs

3. My brother _____ cereal, and I _____ coffee.
    want / wants   **want / wants**

4. The children _____ pizza.
    like / likes

5. Ellen _____ two brothers.
    have / has

6. He _____ a doctor.
    need / needs

7. Tom _____ fish sandwiches.
    like / likes

8. They _____ three children.
    have / has

B. Now circle the correct word.

1. Do you (have / has) a phone number?

2. (Do / Does) the children like hamburgers?

3. He (don't / doesn't) want coffee. He wants tea.

4. What (do / does) you want?

5. Does Joan (need / needs) a new watch?

6. We (don't / doesn't) like coffee.

7. (Do / Does) your brother have children?

8. (Do / Does) you like your new teacher?

9. James (don't / doesn't) like pizza.

10. Do they (want / wants) breakfast?

❸ Write the answers.

Look at the picture. Answer the questions. Use short answers.

1. Do they have milk?   _Yes, they do._
2. Do they have eggs?   _No, they don't._
3. Do they have juice?   _____
4. Do they have cereal?   _____
5. Do they have fish?   _____
6. Do they have rice?   _____
7. Do they have pasta?   _____
8. Do they have bread?   _____

4 Complete the conversations.

Look at the pictures. Complete the sentences with words from the box.

Do	don't	you	~~I'm~~	need	We're	have

Hi, Elaine _____I'm_____
1.
at the supermarket.

Oh, good. _____
2.
out of bread.

Bread... OK. Anything
else? _____ we
3.
need milk?

No, we _____.
4.
We _____ milk.
5.

How about juice? Do we
_____ juice?
6.

Yes, please. And we're out
of rice.

Is that all?

Yes, that's all.
Thanks. See
_____ later.
7.

5 Write the answers.

Answer the questions.

Example: Do you like pizza? _No, I don't._

1. Do you like pizza? _____
2. Do you have coffee for breakfast? _____
3. Do you like milk? _____
4. What drinks do you like? _____
5. Do you eat meat? _____

Challenge

6 Complete the charts.

Complete the sentences in the charts. Use your own words.

For breakfast, I eat
_____
_____
_____ .

I like _____
_____
_____
_____ for lunch.

At night, I eat
_____
_____
_____ .

I don't like _____
_____
_____
_____ .

POWER ACTIVITIES

1 Simple Present Tense

*Write sentences about the people in the pictures. Use **have**, **want**, **need**, and **like**.*

1. ____The girl likes ice cream._____

2. _____

3. _____

4. _____

5. _____

6. _____

2 Mistakes

Find one mistake in each sentence. Then rewrite the sentence correctly.

1. They wants pasta.   ____They want pasta._____

2. He drink coffee.   _____

3. She don't like cereal. _____

4. Max need a book.   _____

5. What do Rachel want?   _____

❸ Things I . . .

*List some things you **like**, **want**, **need**, and **have**.*

Like	Want	Need	Have
basketball	a new car	money	two children

SUPER Challenge

❹ Power Writing: I want a new car!

Write about yourself, your family, and your friends. Write about likes, dislikes, needs, and wants.

_____

_____

_____

_____

_____

_____

_____

Paul always wears jeans.

❶ Complete the chart.

Complete the chart.

	for women	for men	for men and women
a hat			✔
a suit			
a skirt			
a dress			
a tie			
jeans			
a blouse			
a shirt			
a jacket			
socks			

❷ Read and match.

Look at the pictures. Match the pictures and the adjectives.

a. torn

b. loose

c. tight

d. dirty

e. comfortable

f. big

1. ___d.___

2. _____

3. _____

4. _____

5. _____

6. _____

❸ Complete the puzzle.

A. *Look at the pictures. Write the words. Find a new word.*

1.

2.

3.

4.

5.

6.

7.

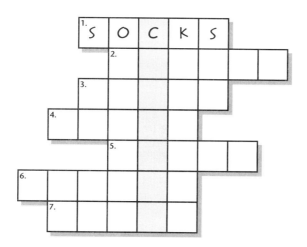

¹S	O	C	K	S	

B. *Now complete the sentence. Use the new word.*

Bella likes black. She usually wears black _____.

Bella looks beautiful today.

4 Label the pictures.

Read about the people. Label the pictures with names from the box.

Mary	Janet	~~Nathan~~	Paul

Nathan is wearing a dirty sweater. His pants are torn. He's not wearing socks.

Paul is a businessman. He's wearing a gray suit with a white shirt and a tie. His black shoes are from Italy. They're expensive.

Maria's wearing a skirt, a white blouse, and a white jacket. Her shoes are new, and they're tight!

Janet always wears jeans and a comfortable sweater. She doesn't wear shoes or socks in the house.

1. ___Nathan___   2. _____   3. _____   4. _____

5 Read and match.

Match the statements and pictures.

a.   b.   c.

d.   e.

1. __e__ "That jacket is beautiful."   4. ____ "Do you like this hat?"

2. ____ "I like that sweater."   5. ____ "Those shoes are ugly!"

3. ____ "These shoes are comfortable."

6 Complete the conversations.

Look at the pictures. Complete the sentences with words from the box.

Are	They're	it	those	~~that~~	It's	they're	Is

I like __that__ **1.** blouse.

_____ **2.** really nice.

_____ **3.** it new?

You do? Thanks!

Yes, _____ **4.** is.

I like _____ **5.** shoes.

Really? Thanks.

_____ **6.** really nice.

_____ **7.** they from Italy?

No, _____ **8.** from Brazil.

7 Complete the sentences.

Complete the sentences with the simple present tense or the present continuous. Use contractions if possible.

1. Maureen ____is wearing____ a beautiful dress today.
   wear

2. My father ____doesn't like____ pizza.
   not like

3. We _____ a dog. His name is Willie.
   have

4. Right now, I _____ juice. I _____ juice every morning.
   drink   **drink**

5. My mother _____ magazines.
   like

6. Rick _____ meat. He never _____ hamburgers.
   not like   **eat**

7. Tony and Paul are in the kitchen. They _____ lunch.
   eat

8. Tom usually _____ a suit.
   wear

9. Today is Sunday. Tom _____ jeans and a sweater.
   wear

10. We _____ bread and milk. We _____ eggs.
   need   **not need**

11. The children _____ TV right now. They always _____ TV at night.
   watch   **watch**

8 Complete the chart.

*Ask a partner. Complete the chart with **usually**, **always**, or **never**.*

Do you . . . . ?

Does your partner . . . . ?

	You	Partner
1. wear clean socks	always	_____
2. watch TV at night	_____	_____
3. drink soda	_____	_____
4. eat breakfast	_____	_____
5. read magazines	_____	_____
6. sleep on the sofa	_____	_____

9 Answer the questions.

Answer the questions with sentences from the box.

Yes, I do.	No, I don't.
Yes, I am.	No, I'm not.

Example: Are you wearing jeans right now? _No, I'm not._

Do you wear jeans on Saturdays? _Yes, I do._

1. Are you wearing jeans right now? _____

2. Do you always wear clean socks? _____

3. Are you hungry right now? _____

4. Are you wearing a tie right now? _____

5. Do you read the newspaper in the morning? _____

6. Do you like coffee? _____

10 Unscramble the words.

Write the questions. Then answer the questions.

1. do / on / Saturdays / What / wear / you

What do you wear on Saturdays ? _I wear jeans._

2. in / coffee / Do / drink / morning / the / usually / you

_____ ? _____

3. a / Are / now / right / sweater / wearing / you

_____ ? _____

4. eat / time / do / lunch / usually / What / you

_____ ? _____

5. doing / are / now / you / What / right

_____ ? _____

POWER ACTIVITIES

❶ Word Groups

Circle the word that is different.

1. sweater   jacket   blouse   (pants)

2. torn   dirty   beige   tight

3. ugly   terrific   nice   beautiful

4. purse   briefcase   shoes   blouse

5. tight   loose   small   short

❷ This / That / These / Those

Complete the sentences. Choose words. Write the words on the line.

1. ____**This**____ hat is black. ____**Those**____ hats are beige.
   This / These   **That / Those**

2. _____ jeans are tight. _____ jeans are loose.
   This / These   **That / Those**

3. _____ shirt is dirty. _____ shirt is clean.
   That / Those   **This / These**

4. I don't like _____ yellow blouse. I like _____ purple blouse.
   that / those   **this / these**

5. We don't want _____ cereal. We want _____ cereal.
   this / these   **that / those**

6. The red sweaters go on _____ shelf. The blue sweaters go on
   that / those

   _____ shelves.
   this / these

❸ Simple Present or Present Continuous?

Write sentences. Use the simple present tense or the present continuous.

1. Lyn / work / Monday through Thursday.

   Lyn works Monday through Thursday. _____

2. Bob / usually / not drink / soda.

   _____

3. Today / I / study / English.

_____

4. He / always / wear / colorful clothes.

_____

5. We / shop / for new jeans / today.

_____

6. They / not eat / right now.

_____

7. What / you / wear / right now?

_____

8. What / you / wear / to school?

_____

9. What / you / wear / on the weekend?

_____

10. What / you / usually / do / on the weekend?

_____

SUPER Challenge

④ Power Writing: Clothes and Activities

Answer questions 7–10 from Exercise 3 for yourself. Use **usually, always,** and **never** where you can.

_____

_____

_____

_____

Take aspirin.

1 Label the pictures.

Label the pictures with words from the box.

arm	back	foot	ear	eye	hand
face	~~head~~	hair	chest	leg	
mouth	nose	teeth	throat	stomach	

1. _head_

2. _____

3. _____

4. _____

5. _____

6. _____

7. _____

8. _____

9. _____

10. _____

11. _____

12. _____

13. _____

14. _____

15. _____

16. _____

❷ Write true or false.

*Look at the picture. Write **T** (true) or **F** (false).*

1. __T__ Ken has a headache.

2. ____ Kathleen's throat hurts.

3. ____ Noah has an earache.

4. ____ Kathleen has a cold.

5. ____ Ken's back hurts.

6. ____ Kathleen has a stomachache.

7. ____ Noah's stomach hurts.

8. ____ Ken's feet hurt.

❸ Unscramble the conversation.

Number the sentences 1, 2, 3, ...

____ 11:30 is fine.

__1__ Doctor's office.

____ I have an earache. I feel terrible.

____ Hello. This is Alice Fitzgerald. I need to see the doctor.

____ How about tomorrow at 11:30?

____ OK. What's the problem, Mrs. Fitzgerald?

____ Good. See you then. Bye.

4 Complete the sentences.

Look at the pictures. Circle the correct words.

1. ((He's)/ She's) looking at (him / her).

2. (He's / They're) looking at (him / her).

3. (They're / She's) looking at (him / them).

4. (He's / She's) looking at (him / her).

5 Complete the sentences.

Complete the conversations with a word from the box.

me	you	~~him~~	her	it	us	them

1. **A:** Where's Paul?

   B: I don't know. I don't see ___*him*___ .

2. **A:** Are you busy?

   B: Well, we're eating dinner right now. Can I call _____ back later?

3. **A:** That's a nice jacket.

   B: Do you want it? I never wear _____ .

4. **A:** How are Anthony and Tina?

   B: I don't know. We never see them, and they never call _____ .

5. **A:** That's Anne.

   B: Anne? I don't know _____ .

6. **A:** Are Karen and Ian hungry?

   B: I don't know. Ask _____ .

7. **A:** What's the matter?

   B: My mother never calls _____ .

6 Read and match.

Complete the conversations. Match the sentences.

1. __c__ You don't look so good. Are you OK?   **a.** I have a fever.

2. _____ Why don't you call the doctor?   **b.** Doctor Park.

3. _____ Who's your doctor?   **c.** No. I feel awful.

4. _____ I feel terrible.   **d.** I'm sorry to hear that.

5. _____ What's the matter?   **e.** Good idea.

7 Read the chart.

Read the chart. Then check (✓) OK or Not OK.

Having A Baby?
Dos and Don'ts

DO	DON'T
• Sleep.	• Work all day.
• Drink water.	• Drink coffee.
• Drink juice.	• Get tired.
• Drink milk.	• Take aspirin.
• Exercise.	

PAUL JONES
M.D.

1.

OK ____

Not OK ✓

2.

OK ____

Not OK ____

3.

OK ____

Not OK ____

4.

OK ____

Not OK ____

5.

OK ____

Not OK ____

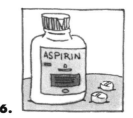

6.

OK ____

Not OK ____

POWER ACTIVITIES

❶ Mistakes

Find one mistake in each sentence. Then rewrite the sentence correctly.

1. Mark son has an earache. <u>Mark's son has an earache.</u>

2. I have thirty-two tooths. _____

3. She is looking at we. _____

4. Scott mother is sick. _____

5. Him feels awful. _____

❷ Grammar Expansion

Complete the sentences. Use possessive nouns, possessive adjectives, object pronouns, and subject pronouns.

1. (The children) Those are ____the children's____ books.

Those are _____their_____ books.

The books belong to _____them_____.

_____They_____ belong to the children.

2. (Mike) That is _____ car.

That is _____ car.

The car belongs to _____.

_____ belongs to Mike.

3. (Sara) These are _____ clothes.

These are _____ clothes.

The clothes belong to _____.

_____ belong to Sara.

4. (The Millers) This is _____ house.

This is _____ house.

The house belongs to _____.

_____ belongs to the Millers.

❸ Imperatives

Complete the sentences. Use imperatives.

Tim has a stomachache.

1. _Don't drink_ _____ milk.

2. _____ tea.

3. _____ ice cream.

4. _____ toast.

5. _____ aspirin.

Jane has a fever and a headache.

6. _____ chicken soup.

7. _____ to bed and _____.

8. _____ outside.

9. _____ aspirin.

10. _____ your doctor.

❹ Power Writing: Ailments and Advice

SUPER Challenge

*Read about the people and their ailments. Give advice. Use ideas from your Student Book and your **own** ideas.*

1. Kathleen has a bad backache.

   Do: ___Stay in bed.___ _____ _____

   Don't: _____ _____ _____

2. Your friend has _____.

   Do: _____ _____ _____

   Don't: _____ _____ _____

3. You have _____.

   Do: _____ _____ _____

   Don't: _____ _____ _____

How was your vacation?

1 Read and match.

Look at the calendar. Match the dates and phrases.

September

Sunday	Monday	Tuesday	Wednesday	Thursday	Friday	Saturday
				1	2	3
4	5	6	7	8	9	10
11	12	13	(14)	15	16	17
18	19	20	21	22		4
25	30					

Today is September 14.

1. __d__ September 13 was
2. ____ September 4–10 was
3. ____ August was
4. ____ September 7 was
5. ____ September 10 and 11 were
6. ____ September 12 was

a. last month.
b. last weekend.
c. two days ago.
d. yesterday.
e. last Wednesday.
f. last week.

❷ Complete the sentences.

Look at the map. Complete the sentences. Use words from the box.

sunny	hot	cloudy	windy
~~raining~~	foggy	snowing	

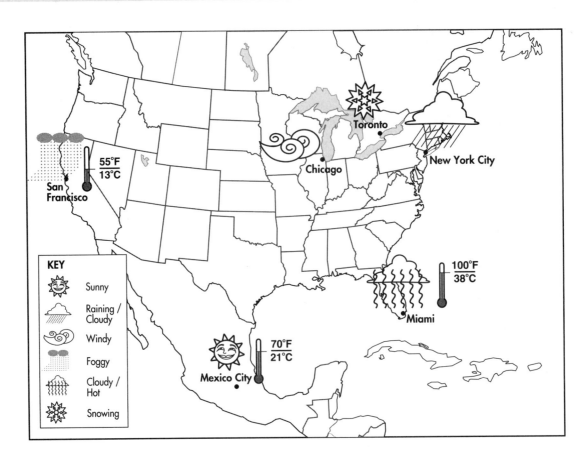

1. It's ___raining___ and _____ in New York.

2. It's _____ in Chicago.

3. It's _____ and _____ in Miami.

4. In San Francisco, it's 55°F (13°C). The weather is cool and _____.

5. In Mexico City, it's _____ and 70°F (21°C).

6. In Toronto, it's _____.

3 Complete the puzzle.

A. Circle seven simple present tense verbs and seven past tense verbs. Words are horizontal (→) or vertical (↓).

O	R	L	W	A	L	P	S	O	P
H	A	V	E	X	E	L	W	R	I
I	N	A	N	T	E	O	A	T	E
I	L	P	T	S	W	I	M	O	R
P	W	H	U	L	I	S	D	O	L
E	T	A	K	E	C	B	I	K	A
R	A	D	L	E	G	A	D	A	M
U	S	L	E	P	T	I	K	U	R
N	O	L	A	R	A	P	G	O	B
L	O	R	T	I	K	L	A	M	D

B. Now write the verbs.

Simple present tense	**Past tense**
do	did
_____	_____
_____	_____
_____	_____
_____	_____
_____	_____
_____	_____

4 Write the sentences.

Write the sentences again. Use the past tense form of the verbs.

1. My teacher is Mike Platt.

   My teacher was Mike Platt.

2. They're very happy.

   They were very happy.

3. Are your sisters at the dance?

   _____

4. The weather is beautiful.

   _____

5. Mark's not here.

   _____

6. My parents are on vacation.

   _____

7. How's the vacation?

   _____

8. You're not my neighbor.

   _____

9. When is the concert?

   _____

10. Where are Barry and Erin?

    _____

5 Read and match.

Match the questions and answers.

1. __c__ How was your vacation?   a. It was warm and sunny.

2. _____ Where did you go?   b. Yes. We took pictures every day.

3. _____ What did you do?   c. Very good!

4. _____ How was the weather?   d. Oh, yes! It was a great vacation.

5. _____ Did you take pictures?   e. We walked and swam and ate good food.

6. _____ Did you have a good time?   f. We went to the mountains.

6 Read and match.

Read the letters.

Letter 1

Dear Pam,

We had a great vacation this year. We went to Hawaii. The weather was beautiful! It was sunny and hot. It only rained at night! We went to the beach, and Bobby and Susan swam every day. The food was very good, too. We had a terrific time, and we took lots of pictures.

Letter 2

Dear Dad,

Last week we went to Paul's house in the mountains. What a place! The house was beautiful. We slept ten hours every night. Every morning, we ate a big breakfast. We went for long walks and played tennis and golf. We didn't watch TV or read the newspaper.

Now match the pictures with the letters. Write Letter 1 or 2.

1. Letter _1_

2. Letter ___

3. Letter ___

4. Letter ___

5. Letter ___

6. Letter ___

7. Letter ___

❶ Grace's Last Vacation

Complete the paragraph about Grace's vacation. Use the simple past tense.

Last month I _____*went*_____ on a great vacation. I _____ to Spain and my
     1. go   **2. travel**

two friends, Christa and Tammy, _____ with me. We _____ lots of
                              3. come   **4. take**

pictures. The weather _____ hot and sunny. Every day we _____ at
                        5. be   **6. swim**

the beach and _____ really good food. Some days we _____ tennis.
             7. eat   **8. play**

At night, we _____ into town and _____ movies at a small theater.
           9. walk   **10. watch**

We _____ so tired at the end of each day that we _____ for nine
   11. be   **12. sleep**

hours every night.

❷ Simple Past Tense

Using the information from Exercise 1, answer the questions. Use complete sentences.

1. When did Grace go on vacation? ___*She went on vacation last month.*___

2. Where did she go? _____

3. Who did she travel with? _____

4. How was the weather? _____

5. What did she do in Spain? _____

_____

6. What did she eat? _____

❸ What's the weather like in the . . . ?

Describe the weather of each season. You can use each word more than once.

sunny	cloudy	windy	foggy	hot
cool	cold	rainy	snowy	warm

Winter	Spring	Summer	Fall
It's cold.			

SUPER Challenge

❹ Power Writing: Your Last Vacation

Answer these questions about the last vacation you took. Use complete sentences.

1. When was your last vacation? _____

_____

2. Where did you go? _____

_____

3. Who did you travel with? _____

_____

4. How was the weather? _____

_____

5. What did you do? _____

_____

6. What did you eat? _____

_____

Unit 10 I'm going to be late.

Challenge

1 Write the answers.

Look at the pictures. Answer the questions with words from the box.

~~a walk~~	dinner	a video	the movies	cards	a party

1. What are Jack and Corrine doing?

   They're taking a walk.

2. What are Janice and Ted doing?

3. What are the men doing?

4. What is Richard doing?

5. What is Ruth doing?

6. What are they doing?

② Read and match.

Look at the calendar. Match the dates and words or phrases.

September

Sunday	Monday	Tuesday	Wednesday	Thursday	Friday	Saturday
11	12	13	Today 14	15	16	17
18	19	20	21	22	23	24
25	26	27	28	29	30	

Today is September 14.

1. __e__ September 17 and 18 are

2. ____ September 15 is

3. ____ September 18–24 is

4. ____ October is

5. ____ September 24 and 25 are

6. ____ September 16 is

a. tomorrow.

b. next month.

c. the day after tomorrow.

d. next weekend.

e. this weekend.

f. next week.

③ Read and match.

Complete the conversations. Match the sentences.

1. __b__ Let's eat out.

2. ____ Let's go to a basketball game on Saturday.

3. ____ What do you want to do next weekend?

4. ____ Let's go to the movies this weekend.

5. ____ It's raining.

6. ____ Do you want to watch TV tonight?

a. No, let's not watch TV. Let's go to the movies.

b. OK. Do you like Japanese food?

c. All right. How about *Star Trax*? It's at the Star Theater.

d. Oh, no! Well, let's not go out.

e. Good idea. I love basketball.

f. Let's have a party!

4 Complete the conversation.

*Complete the sentences. Use **be going to**.*

A: What _____are_____ you _____going to do_____ this weekend?

1. do

B: Oh, this weekend _____ great. Tom and I _____

2. be   **3. take**

a little vacation.

A: Oh, that's nice. _____ you _____ to the country?

4. go

B: Yes. We _____ tennis and sleep. And we _____

5. play   **6. eat out**

at good restaurants. What about you?

A: Oh, I _____ home. Marie and I _____ dinner

7. stay   **8. make**

Saturday night. And then I think we _____ a video.

9. watch

5 Unscramble the conversation.

Number the sentences 1, 2, 3 . . . .

____ I think so. Why?

____ Bye!

____ Eight o'clock.

_1_ Virginia? This is Carol.

____ Hi. Listen, are you free Saturday night?

____ OK. Thanks! See you Saturday.

____ John and I are going to have a party. Would you like to come?

____ Oh, hi, Carol.

____ Sounds good! What time?

6 Unscramble the words.

Write the questions. Then answer the questions.

1. a / going / Are / you / this / take / vacation / year / to

Are you going to take a vacation this year ? _Yes, I am._

2. the / Are / going / next / you / to / weekend / movies / to / go

_____ ? _____

3. tonight / home / going / Are / stay / you / to

_____ ? _____

4. you / to / going / Are / tomorrow / exercise

_____ ? _____

5. are / do / to / What / going / you / weekend / this

_____ ? _____

7 Complete the calendars.

Complete the calendars with your own activities for next week. Write your own dates and times.

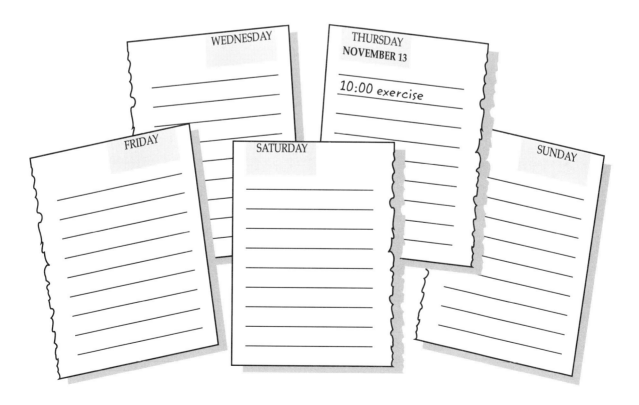

POWER ACTIVITIES

❶ Mistakes

Find one mistake in each sentence. Then rewrite the sentence correctly.

1. Let's taking a walk.   Let's take a walk.

2. I'm go to write a letter.   _____

3. She's going sleep late.   _____

4. What he going to do?   _____

5. We is going to study tomorrow. _____

❷ The Future with *Be Going To*

Look at Beth's calendar for Friday, Saturday, and Sunday. Write about her plans.

Friday	Saturday	Sunday
4:00 p.m. post office	9:00 a.m. gym-swimming	10:00 a.m. take a walk with Pam
9:15 p.m. movies with Jim	10:30 a.m. supermarket	1:00-5:00 p.m. study English
	5:00 p.m. make dinner for the family	7:30 p.m. concert with Jim at Tremont Theater
	7:00 p.m. play cards with Kate and Barry	

1. _Beth is going to go to the post office on Friday._

2. _____

3. _____

4. _____

5. _____

6. _____

7. _____

8. _____

9. _____

3 Suggestions with *Let's*

Match the statements and suggestions. Write the letter on the line.

1. I'm out of milk and coffee. __d__

2. I'm tired. ____

3. I'm hungry! ____

4. It's hot! ____

5. I feel sick. ____

6. I need to exercise. ____

a. Let's take a walk.

b. Let's go to the beach and swim.

c. Let's call the doctor.

d. Let's go to the supermarket.

e. Let's stay home and watch a video.

f. Let's eat lunch.

4 Power Writing: Next Weekend

Write about five things you are going to do next weekend.

1. _____

_____

2. _____

_____

3. _____

_____

4. _____

_____

5. _____

_____

1 Complete the puzzle.

Look at the pictures. Write the words.

CLUES

Across

1.

10.

4.

13.

6.

16.

8.

18.

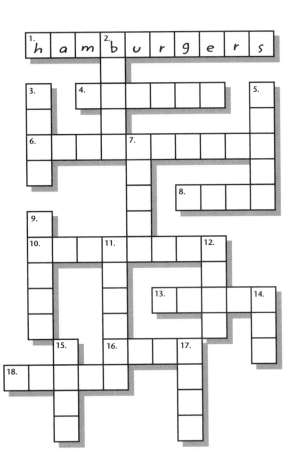

Down

2.

3.

5.

7.

9.

11.

12.

14.

15.

17.

❷ Write the sentences.

Look at the pictures. Write sentences.

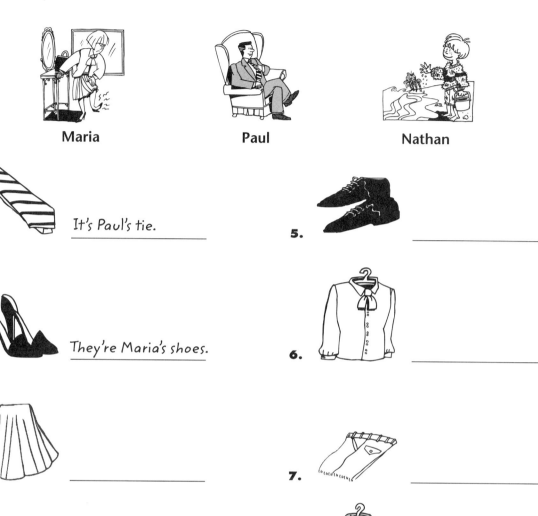

Maria   **Paul**   **Nathan**

1. It's Paul's tie.

5. _____

2. They're Maria's shoes.

6. _____

3. _____

7. _____

4. _____

8. _____

❸ Unscramble the conversation.

Number the sentences 1, 2, 3 . . . .

____ I'm going to go this afternoon.

____ I'm sorry to hear that. What's wrong?

__1__ Hi, Anna! How's it going?

____ Why don't you go to the doctor?

____ I have a fever.

____ Not too good. I feel awful.

4 Write the answers.

Read the letter.

Letters from our Readers:

My name is Elaine Woods. I'm a homemaker from Palo Alto, California. This is my family. My husband, Jack, is a doctor. Peter is our son. He is three years old. Ellen is our daughter. She is five.

Last year I worked in a tall, new office building. I was a writer for a women's magazine.

I'm not working this year because I am really busy at home with my family. We have a lot of family activities.

Next year I'm going to work four days a week. My husband is going to stay home with Peter and Ellen.

*Now complete the sentences with **do**, **does**, or **is**. Then answer the questions. Use capital letters when necessary.*

1. What __is__ the woman's name?   Elaine Woods.

2. What __does__ she do?   She is a homemaker.

3. Where _____ she from?

4. What _____ her husband do?

5. _____ they have a son?

6. _____ she working now?

7. What _____ she going to do next year?

8. _____ they live in Palo Alto, California?

⑤ Complete the sentences.

Complete the sentences with the correct form of the verbs.

1. The weather _____was_____ terrible yesterday.
    be

2. Next Saturday Debra __is going to run__ ten miles.
    run

3. We usually eat at Mario's, but tomorrow night we _____ at Vitello's.
    eat

4. We _____ lots of pictures on vacation last summer.
    take

5. My brother _____ tennis with Harry next week.
    play

6. Yesterday I _____ a bad headache.
    have

7. I _____ in the library tomorrow.
    study

8. It _____ hot last July.
    be

9. It _____ cloudy this weekend.
    be

10. I _____ dinner tomorrow night.
    make

⑥ Complete the charts.

Talk about yourself.

I want	I need	I like
_____	_____	_____
_____	_____	_____
_____	_____	_____
_____	_____	_____
_____	_____	_____
_____	_____	_____

TEST-TAKING SKILLS

SECTION I
Vocabulary You Should Know

1. Read the sentence(s).
2. Try each answer in the space.
3. Circle the letter of the answer that best completes the sentence.

1. He's really hungry. He's eating three _____, soup, and ice cream.

   (A) sandwiches
   (B) pasta
   (C) meat
   (D) pizza

2. We _____ milk and bread. Can you go to the supermarket?

   (A) drink
   (B) have
   (C) don't like
   (D) need

3. I'm thirsty. Is there _____ in the refrigerator?

   (A) juice
   (B) fish
   (C) rice
   (D) soup

4. He wears jeans every day. He _____ wears jeans.

   (A) never
   (B) always
   (C) later
   (D) right now

5. I don't like this skirt. The color is nice, but it's too _____.

   (A) clean
   (B) comfortable
   (C) tight
   (D) new

6. Are you going to wear _____ with your suit?

   (A) a dress
   (B) a sock
   (C) pants
   (D) a tie

7. Louis ate four hamburgers. Now he has a _____.

   (A) toothache
   (B) sore throat
   (C) stomachache
   (D) fever

8. I feel _____. I'm going to sleep early tonight.

   (A) terrific
   (B) thirsty
   (C) hot
   (D) tired

9. Nat usually sings in the shower, but today his _____ hurts.

   (A) back
   (B) foot
   (C) throat
   (D) eye

10. Today is March 28, so March 25 was _____.

    (A) last night
    (B) three days ago
    (C) last month
    (D) three months ago

11. We went to the beach last weekend, but the weather was _____. It was cloudy, raining, and cold.

    (A) terrific
    (B) decent
    (C) pretty good
    (D) terrible

12. What beautiful weather! It's _____ and warm. Let's play golf.

    (A) foggy
    (B) sunny
    (C) windy
    (D) raining

13. We're going to eat out tomorrow night. Tonight let's _____ home and make dinner.

    (A) take
    (B) call
    (C) stay
    (D) buy

14. The dinner party started at 7:00. Rob came at 7:30. He was _____.

    (A) later
    (B) on time
    (C) early
    (D) late

15. Sarah is going to go to Toronto _____. She's going to see her sister.

    (A) last week
    (B) next week
    (C) a week ago
    (D) yesterday

SECTION 2
Vocabulary from Context

> 1. Read the sentence(s).
> 2. Try each answer in place of the underlined word(s).
> 3. Circle the letter of the best answer.

1. Are you thirsty? Do you want a soft drink?

    (A) soda
    (B) toast
    (C) meat
    (D) cereal

2. The fish is not so good here, but the pasta is great. I prefer the pasta.

    (A) make
    (B) am out of
    (C) need
    (D) like

3. When's dinner? I didn't eat lunch, so I'm famished!

    (A) hungry
    (B) awful
    (C) thirsty
    (D) dirty

4. It's going to be a really nice dinner party, Paul. Wear a blazer and a tie.

    (A) dress
    (B) blouse
    (C) watch
    (D) jacket

5. Those hats are ugly, but this one is <u>lovely</u>. I really like it.

   (A) torn
   (B) tight
   (C) beautiful
   (D) dirty

6. Rose has a skirt, a jacket, and shoes for the party, but she still needs a <u>top</u>.

   (A) dress
   (B) blouse
   (C) suit
   (D) sock

7. Nurses see <u>illnesses</u> like colds, fevers, and sore throats almost every day in the winter.

   (A) seasons
   (B) activities
   (C) weather
   (D) ailments

8. Chris works twelve hours a day, and he is always <u>exhausted</u>.

   (A) awful
   (B) terrific
   (C) tired
   (D) hot

9. Kara went to bed early last night. She felt really <u>ill</u>. She had a bad stomachache.

   (A) sick
   (B) terrific
   (C) so-so
   (D) great

10. My parents are from Tokyo. They're here on vacation. They <u>arrived</u> last week.

    (A) started
    (B) ate
    (C) went
    (D) came

11. The weather was <u>miserable</u> last weekend. On Saturday it was cloudy and raining, and on Sunday it was windy and cold.

    (A) decent
    (B) terrible
    (C) terrific
    (D) so-so

12. Anna is working this week, but Harry isn't. He is on a <u>trip</u>. He went to Hawaii for ten days.

    (A) walk
    (B) game
    (C) video
    (D) vacation

13. Dave and his wife went to the mountains last week. It was great. They really <u>enjoyed</u> their vacation.

    (A) played
    (B) liked
    (C) took
    (D) watched

14. I'm going to come home late tonight. Can you <u>prepare</u> dinner?

    (A) have
    (B) take
    (C) make
    (D) eat

15. Elizabeth's tennis class started at 10:00. She came at 10:00. She was <u>prompt</u>.

    (A) on time
    (B) late
    (C) early
    (D) outside

SECTION 3
Sentence Structure

> 1. Read the sentence(s).
> 2. Try each answer in the space.
> 3. Circle the letter of the answer that best completes the sentence.

1. My dad _____ fish. He usually eats it for dinner.

   (A) does he like
   (B) liked
   (C) like
   (D) likes

2. I'm going to the supermarket. What _____ need?

   (A) we
   (B) are we
   (C) do we
   (D) we don't

3. The students _____ soup and sandwiches for lunch today.

   (A) eat
   (B) are eating
   (C) eats
   (D) is eating

4. Don't wear _____ pants. They're torn.

   (A) that
   (B) them
   (C) those
   (D) this

5. Joe works at a gym. He _____ wear a suit to work.

   (A) doesn't
   (B) don't
   (C) wasn't
   (D) isn't

6. Joe _____ a suit today because there's a dance tonight.

   (A) wears
   (B) are wearing
   (C) is wearing
   (D) wear

7. We _____ tennis right now. It's a really good game.

   (A) watching
   (B) watch
   (C) watched
   (D) are watching

8. Doris usually takes a shower in the morning. Her son takes _____ shower at night.

   (A) him
   (B) his
   (C) he
   (D) he's

9. _____ make dinner tonight. I ate a big lunch.

   (A) Don't
   (B) Isn't
   (C) Doesn't
   (D) Do you

10. It was a terrific vacation. They _____ to the beach every afternoon.

    (A) go
    (B) are going
    (C) goes
    (D) went

11. Andrea _____ her sister, but she wasn't at home.

(A) calls
(B) called
(C) calling
(D) doesn't call

12. When _____ going to ask the doctor about her headaches?

(A) she's
(B) is she
(C) is
(D) does she

13. Kevin is sick. He has a fever. Let's call _____.

(A) them
(B) his
(C) he
(D) him

14. _____ Sheila and Tom at the concert last night?

(A) Was
(B) Does
(C) Were
(D) Are

15. I'm really tired. _____ stay home tonight and watch a video.

(A) Let's
(B) Do
(C) Don't
(D) It's

SECTION 4
Error Correction

> 1. Read the sentence.
> 2. Read the underlined words and the words around them.
> 3. Circle the letter below the word that is <u>not</u> correct.

1. Paul <u>like</u> pizza, <u>but</u> he <u>doesn't</u> like pasta, <u>rice</u>, or fish.
       A   B   C   D

2. <u>My</u> sister Jenny <u>doesn't</u> drink <u>coffees</u> or <u>tea</u>.
   A   B   C   D

3. I'm going to <u>buy</u> <u>these</u> dress for the party <u>on</u> Saturday.
    A   B   C   D

4. I <u>don't</u> usually <u>wearing</u> purple, but I <u>love</u> <u>this</u> sweater.
     A   B   C   D

5. Mrs. <u>Clarks</u> skirt <u>is</u> nice, but <u>her</u> blouse is too <u>colorful</u>.
       A   B   C   D

6. <u>That</u> store <u>have</u> very <u>expensive</u> clothes for <u>men</u>.
   A   B   C   D

7. I <u>looked</u> for James <u>at</u> the library, but I <u>didn't</u> see <u>his</u>.
    A   B   C   D

8. Evan <u>were</u> <u>late</u> to work <u>because</u> he had <u>a</u> toothache.
       A   B   C   D

9. <u>Did</u> you <u>played</u> tennis yesterday, or are you <u>going</u> to <u>play</u> next week?
   A   B   C   D

10. The women <u>really</u> <u>loved</u> <u>their</u> vacation <u>at</u> the country last month.
             A   B   C   D

11. Let's <u>playing</u> cards this afternoon <u>because</u> the weather <u>is</u> going <u>to</u> be terrible.
       A   B   C   D

12. Did you <u>take</u> <u>a</u> walk <u>in</u> the mountains yesterday morning, or did you <u>slept</u> late?
           A   B   C   D

13. <u>Call</u> Alicia, but <u>don't</u> ask <u>she</u> about the party at <u>her</u> house on Saturday.
   A   B   C   D

14. <u>Do</u> <u>Molly</u> friends <u>swim</u> <u>at</u> the gym every day?
   A   B   C   D

15. They always <u>play</u> golf on Sunday mornings, but <u>they</u> aren't <u>play</u> this morning
            A   B   C

because <u>it's</u> foggy.
        D